The Surnames Baker & Baxter

Dr Susan Morris
& Wendy Bosberry-Scott

ISBN: 1533589631
ISBN-13: 978-1533589637

The question of surnames, their origins, distribution and history, lies at the heart of genealogy as well as being fascinating in its own right.

In the 1980s and 1990s, long before many genealogical sources were even indexed, let alone online, our Surname Report service provided expert assessments of the origins, history and distribution of selected British surnames, using the sources available at the time.

Now, with so many more sources available, we believe that these reports retain their value as studies of individual surnames, and so we are gradually making the Debrett Surname Archive available online and in print for the first time. Some modern indexes have been consulted to refresh and update the reports.

Debrett Ancestry Research Ltd, PO Box 379,
Winchester SO23 9YQ
Tel: 01962 841904
Email: info@debrettancestry.co.uk
Website: www.debrettancestry.co.uk

CONTENTS

Overview

The use of surnames in England began in the Norman period, when surnames were not necessarily hereditary but usually a form of description. Some described the individual's trade or profession; others were nicknames; some gave the father's Christian name; others gave the individual's place of residence or origin.

Different surnames might be used in different documents, or more than one surname given in one document. Early descriptions were fairly elaborate and by the thirteenth and fourteenth centuries these were simpler, but still variable, and indeed the instability of surnames continued until well into the seventeenth century.

Although some Normans would already have had hereditary surnames on their arrival in Britain, the passing on of a surname from generation to generation only became customary in Britain gradually during the course of the thirteenth and fourteenth centuries. At the end of this period most of the population apparently had surnames.

Variations in the spelling of a family's surname continue to be found until the present century. Before this, as most people could not read or write, the parish clerk or other official would write down the name as they heard it.

There are four main groups of surnames:

> A - Local names, which describe a person by his place of residence or origin.
> B - Occupational names, which describe a person by his trade or profession.
> C - Surnames of relationship, which refer to the Christian name of the father or other important relative.
> D - Nicknames or sobriquets, coined to describe a person in terms of his appearance or character.

Many surnames have uncertain origins, but the name Baker clearly falls into Category B and would originally have been given to one who was a baker (in Old English *bæcere*).

Origins and Early Examples

The name Baker has been found in several variant forms during the course of our research, including Baiker, and Backer. The surname Baxter is its female partner: it has the same root but is the feminine form and therefore a separate surname. The variants of Baxter we have found are Bagster and Baxster.

The surname Baker is listed in *A Dictionary of English Surnames* by the late P H Reaney and R M Wilson (1995), where the following medieval incidences of the surname are shown:

1177	William le Bakere	Norfolk Pipe Rolls
1246	Robert Bakere	Lancashire Assizes
1280	Walter le Backere	Hampshire

The Hampshire example was taken from G Fransson's *Middle English Surnames of Occupation 1100-1350* (Lund, 1935).

W J Hardy and W Page's *Calendar to the Feet of Fines for London and Middlesex 1189-1485,* provides a useful list of medieval surnames; by the end of the fifteenth century, a very large proportion of English surnames had found their way to London. The fine was a means of conveying or settling freehold property, from the reign of Richard I up to 1834, when a Statute was passed to abolish the method and set up a simpler way of achieving matters.

Here we find six references to the surname Baker.

> John le Waruner, of Kenyngton and **Thomas le Bakere**, of Certeseye, and Gunnulda his wife. Premises in Reye and Feltham Anno 33 Edward I [circa 1305]

> **Henry le Bakere**, and Joan, his wife, and John Bythewode, and Juliana, his wife. Land in Colham. Anno 7 Edward III [circa 1334]

> Edmund Lannar, and Olive, his wife, and John, son of **William le Bakere**, of Haveryng. Premises in Fynchesle. Anno 10 Edward III [circa 1337]

> Philip Plumtre, and Amicia, his wife, and **John Baker**, of London, cordwainer, and Matilda, his wife. A messuage in Eye. Anno 31 Edward III [circa 1358]

> Nicholas Toller, citizen and skinner of London, and Richard Toller, and Elizabeth, his wife, John Toller, **Ralph Baker**, John Edmet, and James Clyfton. Premises in Stanwell. Anno 9 Henry VI [circa 1431]

> **Thomas Baker**, Matilda, widow of John Veysour, and John Kyng, and Thomas ate Hacche, and Alice, his wife. Land in Willesdon. Anno 15 Henry VI [circa 1437]

At the beginning of the fourteenth century we find the surname with the article 'le' denoting an occupational name. By the end of that same century this has been dropped and we find the surname just as Baker.

All the major surname scholars have had something to say about the surname Baker and its associated form Baxter.

M A Lower, author of *Patronymica Brittanica* (1860), a very early surname dictionary, did not have the benefit of modern research but his comments are often interesting. He made the following observations on the surname Baker and its associated forms and was the first to point out the relevance of the name Baxter:

> **Backer** – The same as Backman (Lower shows the meaning of Backman as 'one who had the care of a back or ferry'.)
> **Bagster** – the same as Baxter
> **Baker** – The occupation. In old documents, Pistor, Le Baker, &c.
> **Baxter** – The Old English and Scottish form of Baker. See termination -STER.
> [example] John le Bakestere Hundred Rolls

The reference to 'see termination STER' is explained as:

> An Anglo Saxon termination, denoting some feminine occupation, as ER does a masculine one, as spinner, spinster. Many of the surnames with this desinence show the change of English customs in regard to the employments of women within the past few centuries: for example, brewing, baking, and weaving were formerly feminine labourers, and consequently Brewster, Baxter, Webster mean the woman (not the man) who brews, bakes or weaves. How these feminine words became transferred to the other gender, so as to become hereditary as surnames, is explained by Mr Poulson, in his Beverlac, p 128 – 'when men began to invade those departments of industry by which women used to earn an honest livelihood, they retained the feminine appellation for some

5

time, as men-midwives and men-milliners now do; but afterwards masculine words drove the feminine ones out of the language, as men had driven the women out of the employments'.

Forty years later, the Victorian scholar C W Bardsley in his *Dictionary of English and Welsh Surnames with Special American Instances* (1901) mentions Baker and Baxter and several variants of both surnames as follows:

Backer occupational, 'the baker'
1466   'To … the backers wyffe, for v mennes borde.'

(Historical English Dictionary)
1547   James Bacar and Hungerford [sic]
        Allegations for Marriage Licences issued from
        the Faculty Office of the Archbishop of Canterbury
1591   Edward Baccar Calendar of State Papers (Domestic)

Post Office, London Commercial Directory 1870 – Backer 2

James Gospill & Sons, *Philadelphia* 1885 – Backer 4

Backster, Bagster, Baxter occupational 'the bakester' a baker of bread, with the feminine suffix; originally a woman's occupation.
Langland speaks of: Baksteres and brewesteres, And bochiers manye'

Baxter, bakstare, baker: *Promptorium Parvulorum* (editor Albert Way, Camden Society, 1865) p 21
Backster is one of the names in Foxe's list of Marian martyrs.

The ordinances of the Guild of the Purification (Bishop's Lynn, 1367), are signed by Johannes Austyn, baxter (English Guilds, p 90).

Capgrave says 'In this same tyme (BC 205) lyved the eloquent man which hite [was called] Plautus, and for al his eloquens he was compelled for to dwell with a Baxter, and grind his corne at a querne'

1273	Giliana le Bacster	Hampshire Assizes
1273	John le Bakestere	Norfolk Assizes
1302	Elias le Baxtere	Writs of Parliament
	Bartholomew le Bakestere	Calendariu Inquisitions Post Mortem
	Andrew le Bakester	Calendarium rotulorum Originalium
1379	Agnes Bakestere	Poll tax, Yorkshire
1379	Cecilia Bakester	*ibid*
1430	William Mytton, backester	Surtees, *Visitations of Yorkshire*

Patrick Adamson (1537-92), a Scotch prelate 'His enemies taunted him with being a baker's son, "ane baxter's sone"' (*Dictionary of National Biography*)

1622   Thomas Smith, backster   Preston Guild Rolls

Post Office London Commercial Directory 1870 – Bacster 0, Bagster 2, Baxter 56

Wilson *New York Directory* 1877 – Bacster 1, Bagster 0, Baxter 0

James Gospill & Sons *Philadelphia Directory* 1885 – Bacster 0, Bagster 0, Baxter 99

Bagster occupational 'the baxter'
Variant - Backster

Baker occupational 'the baker'
Variants – Backster, Baxter

1273	Walter le Baker	Devon Assizes
1273	William le Bakere	Oxford Assizes
1273	Alan le Baker	Sussex Assizes
1 Edw III (1327/8) John le Baker		*Kirby's Quest for Somerset* ... (Somerset Record Society, 1889)
	Roger le Baker	*ibid*
1555	Jane Baker	baptismal record St Peter Cornhill [London]

Post Office London Commercial Directory 1870 – Baker 272

James Gospill & Sons *Philadelphia Directory* 1885 – Baker 420

Baxter occupational 'a female baker', a bakester
Variant – Backster

Ernest Weekley also commented on the pairing of Baker and Baxter in *The Romance of Surnames* (1914):

> [Baker] is reinforced by Bullinger, French *boulanger*, Pester, Old French *pestour* (Latin Pistor) and Furner –

Fournier, a baker, or one that keeps, or governs, a common oven (Cotgrave – A Dictionarie of French and English Tongues (London 1611)) ....

The ending –ster was originally feminine, and applied to trades chiefly carried on by women, eg Baxter, Bagster, Baker, Brewster, Simister, Sempster, Webster etc, but in process of time the distinction was lost, so that we find Blaxter and Whitster for Blacker, Blaker and Whiter, both of which, curiously enough, have the same meaning –

Bleykester or whytster, candidarious (Promptoriun Parvulorum editor Mayhew)

for this black represents Middle English *blāc*, related to bleak and bleach, and meaning pale.

The modern authority P H Reaney had the following to say about the name Baxter:

Baxter, Bagster OE *bæcestre* feminine form of *bæcere* 'baker'. Baxter is found mainly in the Anglian counties and is used chiefly of men. Only two examples have been noted with a woman's Christian name.
abt 1093   Liueger se Bacestere Devon
(G Tengvik *Old English Bynames* (Upsalla, 1938))

1260   Hanne Bakestre   Assize Rolls
                                                      Cheshire
1333   William le Baxtere   Feet of Fines Suffolk
(Reaney & Wilson, *A Dictionary of English Surnames* (Oxford 1995))

Baker is thus a separate surname to Baxter but has the same etymological root. We were to find that, although the two

9

surnames are common in England, Baker was the dominant form but Baxter was, in the early years, more common in certain areas of England than Baker.

In a separate work, *The Origins of the English Surnames* (1967), Reaney expands further on the surname:

> Just as the peasant was not allowed to grind his corn where he wished, so he was forbidden to bake his bread at home or anywhere save in a special oven constructed for the purpose and belonging to the lord. Many peasants had no means of baking at home. The lord's oven was generally rented to an individual or to the peasants as a body. The village oven or bakehouse was a communal convenience (H S Bennett, *Life on the English Manor* (Cambridge 1938) page 135). Hence we have not only the common surnames Baker and Baxter but also Ovens.
>
> John Attenouene (1276 – Somerset Assizes), from Old English *ofen* oven, Backhouse, Bacchus, Backus, Robert ate bachus (1289 – Calendar of Norwegian Deeds) 'worker at the bakehouse', with the French Bullinger, Pullinger and Pillinger (Old French *boulengier* 'baker'), Furner and Fournier (Old French *furnier*) and Pester, Pistor (Anglo-French Pestour, Pistour, Latin Pistor).
>
> Like the Smith, the baker is found in towns too, congregating in such streets as Baxter Street in Bury St Edmunds.

Reaney again treats Baker and Baxter as separate surnames and mentions other associated names. We were to find one of these, Pistor, in some of the records we examined during this research.

Patrick Hanks' & Flavia Hodges' broader-based *Dictionary of Surnames* (Oxford, 1992), which includes names of European derivation, includes the following entry:

> **Baker** English: occupation name, from ME *bakere*, OE *bæcere*, a derivative of *bacan* to bake. It may have been used for someone whose special task in the kitchen of a great house or castle was the baking of bread, but since most humbler households did their own baking in the Middle ages, it may also have referred to the owner of a communal oven used by the whole village. The right to be in charge of this and exact money or laves in return for its use was in many parts of the country a hereditary feudal privilege. Less often the surname may have been acquired by someone noted for baking particularly fine bread or by a baker of potter or bricks.
>
> *Variants*: English Baiker, Bacher, Baxter (originally a feminine form common especially in East Anglia).
> *Cognate*: German – Bäcker, Becker, Beckermann. Flemish, Dutch – Bakker, de Ba(e)cker, de Becker, Bakmann. Jewish (Ashkenazic) – Be(c)ker(man).
> *Patronymic*: Flemish, Dutch – Beckers
> *Equivalents*: French – Boulanger, Fournier. German – Pfister. Polish – Kołacz, Piekarski. Russian – Khlebniko. Hungarian – Liszt.

The modern surname scholar R A McKinley, in his *History of British Surnames* (Longman, 1990), comments further on the feminine form of the name:

> Some occupational surnames, including some quite common ones, exist in pairs: examples are Baker and Baxter ...

11

The reasons for the existence of such names has been the subject of much debate among the experts, but the general conclusion has been that names such as Baxter, Brewster, Webster, and so forth were originally from the feminine forms of occupational terms, while names such as Baker, Brewer or Webber, were from masculine ones. In some parts of southern England names such as Baxter, Brewster, or Webster were still mainly the surnames or more often the by-names, of women during the thirteenth and fourteenth centuries, but even in these areas they were already being used as the name of men by about 1200. In most parts of England there are examples of names such as Baxter, Brewster, etc, appearing as men's names during the thirteenth century. In southern Scotland, too, such names occur as those of men at the same period.

Since some surnames are derived from feminine first names, and since until after 1400 instances can be found of surnames in all categories descending hereditarily through females, it is quite possible that some surnames such as Baxter, Brewster, etc originated with women and were inherited from them by their descendants. Women are inadequately represented in most historical sources, and there is generally much less evidence about their surnames or by-names than about men's. It is consequently quite possible that names such as Baxter, etc were considerably more common as women's names than would appear from the existing written sources.

McKinley goes on to conclude that, since surnames such as Baxter and Brewster, whose origins were apparently feminine, are all fairly common today whereas other, similar, surnames, whose origins were also from the feminine form, are mostly scarce. McKinley argues that this is probably due:

... to the fact that the descent of surnames from females was always the exception, and that in some parts of England names in this group were still predominantly those of women in the thirteenth and fourteenth centuries, when many occupational names were becoming hereditary.

Distribution

The existing volumes of the English Surname Series (which is very incomplete) show several references to Baker etc. In *The Surnames of Lancashire*, the author, Richard McKinley, states that Baker, as an occupational surname, is rare in Lancashire despite its popularity elsewhere in England. The variant Baxter, which belongs to another group of surnames rare in Lancashire (those ending in –(e)ster) he found to be more numerous in its appearances that other surnames in this group. He found that, on a national basis, Baxter was only found in small number before 1500 and that most of the Lancashire examples appear in the south of that county. In the Protestation Returns of Salford for the year 1642, he found only ten persons named Backster or Baxter amongst the more than 13,000 listed.

Detailed studies have also been published on the surnames of Sussex, Oxfordshire and Norfolk and Suffolk in this series. In the volume dealing with Sussex surnames, McKinley reports that occupational names in that county account for some 18 to 20 per cent of the total of surnames appearing. He found Baker to be amongst the most common of this group, being widespread in Sussex as early as the thirteenth century. Its location within the county was found to be so scattered in the records he consulted (Subsidy Rolls from 1296, 1327 and 1332) that he concluded that the appearance of Baker as a surname in Sussex could not be attributed to a single family. He examined Lay Subsidy Rolls (a list of tax-payers) for 1327 and 1332, for a selection of English counties, and compared the numbers of appearances of selected surnames in each county. Baker was one of those chosen:

Subsidy Rolls

Appearances of the name Baker

County	Date	Numbers per thousand
Dorset	1327	3
Kent	1334/5	6.5
Lancashire	1332	1
Leicestershire	1327	1
Oxford	1327	3
Staffordshire	1327	2
Suffolk	1327	2.5
Surrey	1332	6.5
Sussex	1332	5.5
Warwickshire	1327	3.5

As can be seen, the highest numbers appear in the south-eastern counties of Kent, Surrey and Sussex. Unlike other occupational surnames, Baker is more common in some areas of England than others and McKinley comments that Baxter was more common in the north and north-east of the country. McKinley also cites one example of the Latin form of the surname: John Pistor Witegrom (Indelwick, Winchelsea) who appears in the records in 1292. His double surname may have been an attempt to distinguish him from another man with the same personal name and by-name, particularly as there were other men in Winchelsea, at the same time, who were named Pistor.

In the Oxfordshire volume, McKinley found Baxster to be one of the more common occupational names. He first found it recorded in Oxfordshire at the end of the fourteenth century and in Oxford itself in the fifteenth century, when several members of the university were named Baxter, but none appeared to be native to Oxfordshire. In Suffolk and Norfolk McKinley found Baker to be common from the late thirteenth century onwards and occurring widely in the twelfth and early thirteenth centuries, either as Baker or its Latin equivalent Pistor. In general, he found Baxter to be the more common form of the name in Norfolk and Suffolk than Baker and noted that the suffix –*ster* was more common in those counties, when referring to occupational names, than in other counties.

David Postles, author of *The Surnames of Devon*, cites Alice la Bakeres, who was fined in the manors of Longbridge Deverill and Monkton Deverill in 1307, as one of a number of women – probably widows or daughter – bearing bynames with the genitival 's' (indicating 'son/daughter of'). Few men were found with similar names in this area. In the fourteenth century he found Cecily Bakestere in Barnstaple (in north Devon) and Edward Bagester in Exeter, south-east of Barnstaple, in the sixteenth century. He concludes that Edward may well have been an immigrant into Devon as '...this sort of byname was not usually associated with males in Devon'. Postle includes a chart showing a list of occupational surnames and bynames taken from tax records of 1332. Where the total taxpayers numbered 10614, there were 290 Baker, 20 Pistor and 50 Pestour entries.

Conducting a similar survey for *The Surnames of Leicestershire and Rutland*, David Postles found that, in late thirteenth and fourteenth century tax records, the suffix –*ster* was restricted to four particular occupational bynames and surnames, one of which was Baxter and its variants. As Leicester and Rutland are not far from Norfolk, where this suffix was most commonly used, this is perhaps not surprising. He did not, however, find any examples of the surname Baker or any other occupational surname without this suffix. However, in 1327 he found eleven taxpayers recorded in a lay subsidy with an occupational surname using the suffix *–ster*, including seven Baxters. He also found one example of Bakar, at Market Bosworth, which lies in the west of Leicestershire and this appeared to be a commonality in this area as other aberrant forms of such surnames (without the additional *–ster*) were all found in this area.

In the mid-fourteenth century (1341) Postles found Ba(u)xters recorded in the tenancy records of Leicester Abbey at Thurmaston, Lockington and Thornton, but no Bakers. He did, however, find Baker recorded in the court rolls of Breedon in 1362 and in a rental of Loughborough in 1370. These isolated incidences, he concludes, may well be due to an influence from the north of the county. He found that the name Baker had become more common by the late middle ages, perhaps through immigration into the county from elsewhere. In the neighbouring, and smaller, county of Rutland, he found incidences of Baker in the early sixteenth century records of Uppingham, Caldecott, Braunston, Morcott, Burley, Cottesmore, Whissendine and Ridlington; a significant widespread distribution across this small county. Postles' work seems to suggest that the name Baker was found in Leicestershire in significant numbers in the early fourteenth century but not in Rutland until the early fifteenth century. The form Baker or Bakar, he found, was consistent in Leicester itself from the mid-thirteenth century up to the early sixteenth century with a single occurrence of de Pistrina in 1286, and Pistor or Pestour occurring between 1207 and 1341 (fourteen appearances in total).

George Redmond, author of the study of surnames in *Yorkshire, West Riding*, found surprisingly few mentions of the name Baker etc but he does give one example of Bakster which clearly shows its derivation:

> 1436   John Alethorp alias Bakster, son of John
>   Alethorp, bakster

Redmond states that in the larger urban communities of West Yorkshire many names were still not hereditary in the fifteenth century, particularly when a son broke with tradition and decided to follow a different trade from that of his father. This could be true in this instance: John Alethorp senior was a baker his son John was known as John Alethorp and John Bakster. Redmond found the surname Baker recorded in the Poll Tax returns for 1379 in Swillington (which lies to the east of Leeds).

Although the word Baker is of Old English origin, we consulted two works on Norman immigrants, Avenel's *The Norman People* (1975) and L G Pine's *They Came With The Conqueror* (1954), because there was evidence of the usage of the name in Norman families. There was no reference to the surname or any of its variants in L G Pine's work, but in *The Norman People* there is an entry for Baker as follows:

> **Baker** derived from:
> 1. the feudal office of Pistor Regis

18

2. from the tenure of lands
3. in later times from trade

1086   Osmond Pistor Regis who held Windestorte
        and Galton was ancestor of the Bakers of Dorset
        (Domesday)
1086   Those of Devon descended from Erchanger
        Pistor a Norman, who held lands in Somerset and
        Cambridge (Domesday)
1130   Those of Kent from Radulphus Pistor, who
        possessed estates in Surrey (Rotulus ?Cancellarii)
1180   Geoffry, Richard, William and Peter Pistor
        occur in Normandy (Magn. Rotul. Scaccarri
        Normanniae in the Mémoires de las Société des
        Antiquaires de la Normandie)

Pine asserts that at least two large families in Dorset and Devon named Baker descended from Norman immigrants named Pistor or who held the post of Pistor.

In 1890 H B Guppy published his *Homes of Family Names in Great Britain*, still the only published work on surname distribution in Britain as a whole. His work was based on printed genealogies and a survey of county directories for the 1880s, in which he looked especially at the names of farmers, reasoning that they were among the most stable groups in society.

Guppy restricted his study to names which appeared in a proportion of 7:10,000 or higher. We were not surprised to find that he mentioned both Baker and Baxter. However, Guppy did not mention any other variant of this surname; indicating their rarity.

19

Baker

Bedfordshire	18
Buckinghamshire	18
Cheshire	14
Cornwall	20
Devon	58
Dorset	20
Durham	16
Essex	54
Gloucestershire	30
Hampshire	51
Herefordshire	20
Kent	36
Lancashire	16
Leicestershire & Rutland	25
Lincolnshire	15
Monmouthshire	110
Norfolk	24
Northamptonshire	25
Nottinghamshire	28
Oxfordshire	20
Somerset	88
Staffordshire	16
Suffolk	51
Surrey	70
Sussex	80
Warwickshire	30
Wiltshire	30
Worcestershire	14
Yorkshire N & E	10

Baxter

Lincolnshire	9
Yorkshire W	9

As can be seen, Baker is by far the dominant of the two surnames. Guppy also states:

> Speaking generally, this surname [Baker] is most numerous in the south of England, and diminishes rapidly in frequency as we proceed northward, until we reach the counties bordering Scotland, where it meets its extinction within sight of the Cheviot Hills. Baker is a name which prefers the coast; and the manner in which it abounds in almost all the coast counties of southern England (excluding Cornwall and Dorset), from Monmouth round to Suffolk, is very remarkable, and not at first sight intelligible. The counties of Monmouth, Somerset, Sussex and Surrey stand foremost amongst those containing the greatest number of Bakers.

We consulted George F Black's *The Surnames of Scotland* (1966) in which we found the following entry for Baxter (other variants and the surname Baker were not provided with a separate entry in this work):

> **Baxter** This surname comes from the occupation of 'bakester', originally a woman that baked, Old English *bæcestre* a female baker. In Middle English the ending – estre being unstressed soon lost its final e, and –ster came to be regarded as an emphatic form of –er, and consequently was applied to men as well as women, so that the early Middle English feminine *bakstere* became later Middle English masculine *baxster*. Baxter was and still is a common surname in Angus, and as Forfar was a royal residence the first Baxters there may have been the royal bakers. In Latin charters the word or name is

21

rendered *pistor*. [Variants] Bacster 1533, Bakster 1467, Baxstar 1505, Baxstair 1506, Baxstare 1531, Baxster 1512.

Between 1153 and 1177
William *pistor* witnessed a grant by David Olifard to the Hospital of Soltre (soltre p 4)

circa 1188-1202 – Aldred *pistor* was one of the witnesses to a charter of the kirk of Haddington (RPSA p153).

Between 1200 and 1240 – Reginald Baxtar witnessed the gift of the church of Wemys in Fife to Soltre (Soltre p13).

1296 – Geffrei le Baxtere of Lossithe of the County of Forfare took the oath of fealty (Bain ii p 208).

1312 – William Baxtare was a crossbowman in Edinburgh Castle (Bain ii p 409)

1323 – Thomas dictus Baxter, burgesss of Irvine, made a grant for support of a chaplain in the parish church of Irvine (Irvine i 123)

c1330 – Hutredus *pistor* was burgess of Roxburgh (Kelso, 369)

1398 – Robert Baxter was a town official in Aberdeen (CRA p 375)

In Edward MacLysaght's *Guide to Irish Surnames* (1965) and *The Surnames of Ireland* (1973) we found the following entries:

Baker. An English name found in all the provinces. It was in Ireland, as le Bakere, as early as the thirteenth century.

Baxter. Quite numerous in Ulster this name came from Scotland where Mac an Bhacstair is a branch of the Clan MacMillan. [Baxter is an old word for Baker (1973)]

MacLysaght has distinguished the presence of both surnames in Ireland as immigrants from England (Baker) and Scotland (Baxter).

We also consulted T J Morgan and Prys Morgan's *Welsh Surnames* (1985), but found nothing for Baker, Baxter, etc. In his *A History of British Surnames* (Longman 1990, p 150) McKinley states that:

> In Wales a high proportion of surnames, including many of the more common ones, are derived from personal names, and no occupational names from the Welsh language are as common as names such as Smith, Baker, Clark, and so on are in English.

Finally, we consulted J J Kneen's, *The Personal Names of the Isle of Man* (Oxford, 1937), and found the following entries for Baker and Baxter:

Baker [bɛː'ker] English

1730	Baker	Registers of St Mary's Ballure, and St Paul's Ramsey
1748	Baker	Registers of St Matthew's, Douglas
1764	Baker	*ibid*
1767	Baker	Monumental Inscriptions, Maughold

Meaning - A baker
Variant - Baxter

From Statute Laws of the Isle of Man (Mills, 1852)

'Alsoe that the Comptroller be every Saturday at the Peele, and take the Household as he will answer unto me, and take the Steward, the Cooke, the Brewer and Baker, and charge them on their oaths to give a true Expence for the Week past; and this to be done upon Paine of forfeiting his Fees. And in the same Manner every Sunday at Castle Rushen' AD 1422

Baxter [baks'ter] English
1783   Baxter   Monumental Inscriptions, Malew
Meaning - A woman or female baker

Baker seems to have been the most common of the two surnames on the island but neither apparently appears as a surname in the records before the eighteenth century.

Many of the sources available for charting surname distribution through the centuries are necessarily confined to the wealthier sectors of the population: in general, nobody wanted to know the names of the poor but the names of those with money or land were naturally of interest to the authorities. However, one source that covers the whole of the social spectrum is provided by English parish registers, the earliest of which began in 1538 following a mandate that all parish priests should keep a weekly record of all baptisms, marriages and burials that took place in their parish. A survey of a cross section of parish registers for the years 1601 and 1602 was carried out in 1910 by F K and S Hitching; incidences of a particular surname are noted by parish and county, although with no indication of numbers of references.

We looked for entries for the surname Baker and Baxter and any possible variant of the two surnames. The following entries were found:

1601

Backer
Dutch Church, Austen Friars, London

Baker
Reading, St Mary, Berkshire
St Sepulchre's, Cambridgeshire
Sandiacre, Derbyshire
Barnstaple, Devon
Esh, County Durham
King's Stanley, Gloucestershire
Standish, Gloucestershire
Church Oakley, Hampshire
Burnley, Lancashire
St Mary, Woolnoth, London
St Mary, Woolchurch Haw, London
St Helen's Bishopsgate, London
St Martin's in the Fields, London
Spalding, Lincolnshire
Heacham, Norfolk
Stoke Bruerne, Northamptonshire
Sutton in Ashfield, Nottinghamshire
Whittingdon, Shropshire
Oswestry, Shropshire
Rattlesdon, Suffolk
Kingsbury Episcopi, Somerset
Taunton, St Mary Magdalene, Somerset
Walsall, St Matthew, Staffordshire
Barton under Needwood, Staffordshire
Hamstall, Staffordshire
Godalming, Surrey

Bakers
Almer, Dorset

Baxter
St Alban's Abbey, Hertfordshire
St Vedast, Foster Lane, London
Manchester Cathedral, Lancashire
Denham, Suffolk
Ickworth, Suffolk
Walsall, Staffordshire
Barton under Needwell, Staffordshire
Linton in Craven, Yorkshire

1602
Baker
Reading St Mary, Berkshire
Padstow, Cornwall
Barnstaple, Devon
Maisemore, Gloucestershire
St Martin in the Fields, London
St Botoloph, Bishopsgate, London
Walton on the Hill, Lancashire
Clerkenwell St James, Middlsex
Maxey, Northamptonshire
Hughley, Shropshire
Ludlow, Shropshire
Oswestry, Shropshire
Frostenden, Suffolk
Rattlesden, Suffolk
Martock, Somerset
Shepton Beauchamp, Somerset
Crewkerne, Somerset
Taunton St Mary Magdalene, Somerset
Walsall, Staffordshire

Hamstall Ridware, Staffordshire
Haslemere, Surrey
Stratford on Avon, Warwickshire
Newton Tony, Wiltshire

Baxter
St Alban's Abbey, Hertfordshire
St Vedast, Foster Lane, London
Colne, Lancashire
Manchester Cathedral, Lancashire
Glinton, Northamptonshire
Bardwell, Suffolk
Barton under Needwood, Staffordshire
Bolton by Bolland, Yorkshire

As can be seen, in both years Baker was by far the most widespread of the surnames noted. Baxter is found in the middle and north east of England whereas Baker is more scattered across the whole of the country.

Scottish records of births, baptisms, marriages and deaths are now indexed online for the period 1553 to 1953. Using this index we found the following entries for the name Baker (etc) and also checked for Baxter and its variants:

Old Parish Register Index of Births & Christenings 1553-1854

Backer	2
Bagster	1
Baiker	3
Baker	134
Baxster	53
Baxter	8130

Statutory Registration Index to Births 1855-1904

Backer	12
Baiker	1
Backer	817
Baxter	7771

Old Parish Registers Index of Banns & Marriage 1553-1854

Backer	4
Bagster	1
Baker	202
Baxster	37
Baxter	4976

Statutory Registration Index to Marriages 1855-1929

Backer	6
Baker	860
Baxter	5576

Statutory Registration Index to Deaths 1855-1954

Backer	12
Baiker	1
Baker	1378
Baxster	1
Baxter	10864

Although there are high numbers of entries for the Baker surname Baxter is by far the more dominant surname.

A useful guide to the distribution of surnames for the sixteenth, seventeenth and eighteenth centuries in England is provided by the indexes to wills proved, and administrations granted, at the Prerogative Court of (the Archbishop of) Canterbury, in London, which had superior jurisdiction over local ecclesiastical courts where wills were proved until 1858.

The PCC thus provides a national index, although it is not a completely representative one, as testators whose wills were proved in the PCC were mostly among the wealthier members of society, and a disproportionate number of them were from London or Middlesex. A search of the online index found no entries for the name Baiker. As expected, there were a great number of entries for the names Baker and Baxter and so we have shown the number for each period only, but we noted the following entries for (de) Backer, Bagster and Baxster:

Fifteenth Century 1400-1499
London
    Baxster   1

Sixteenth Century 1500-1599
Cambridgeshire
    Baxster   1
Dorset
    Backer   1
London
    Baxster   3
Norfolk
    Baxster   1
Unknown
    Baxster   1   [or Baxter]

Seventeenth Century 1600-1699
Cornwall
    Backer   1
Dorset
    Backer   1
Hertfordshire
    Backer   1

Kent
   Backer   1
Leicestershire
   Baxster   1   [or Baxter]
London
   de Backer   1
Middlesex
   Bagster   2
Somerset
   Backer   1
Staffordshire
   Baxster   1
Unknown
   de Backer   2
   Backer   1
   Baxster   1   [or Baxter]
Wiltshire
   Backer   1   [or Baker]
Worcestershire
   Baxster   1
Mariner
   Backer   2   [or Baker]

Eighteenth Century 1700-1799
Dorset
   Bagster   1
Hampshire
   Bagster   4
Hertfordshire
   Backer   5
Holland
   Backer   21
   de Backer   1
Isle of Wight
   Bagster   1

Kent
 Bagster 1
London
 Backer 2
Middlesex
 Bagster 2
Sussex
 Bagster 2
Unknown
 Backer 1
Yorkshire
 Bagster 1
Mariner
 Bagster 2
New England
 Backer 1

Nineteenth Century 1800-1899
Berkshire
 Bagster 1
Hampshire
 Bagster 1
Holland
 Backer 6
London
 Bagster 1
Middlesex
 Backer 1
 Bagster 5
Surrey
 Bagster 1
Unknown
 Backer 1

Baker

Date range	Numbers of Testators
1400-1499	19
1500-1599	157
1600-1699	697
1700-1799	988
1800-1899	1126

Baxter

Date Range	Numbers of Testators
1500-1599	10
1600-1699	94
1700-1799	138
1800-1899	154

As we can see, Baker is again the dominant surname but we can see that both surnames and their variants were found in all areas of south-east England.

At least three of these entries showed that the testator was known as Baker or Backer: William Backer or Baker was a gunner's mate on the ship *Comfort*; his will was proved in September 1635. Edward Baker or Backer, a yeoman of Keevil in Wiltshire, had his will proved in July 1659. Finally, Edward Backer or Baker, another mariner, this one belonging to 'their Majesty's ship *Burford*' had his will proved in September 1692. We also found George Baxter, otherwise Bagster, a mariner whose will was proved in May 1760.

Index to Scottish testaments (wills) are available online and, using this index, we noted the following:

Scottish Wills & Testaments 1513-1901

Name	Numbers of Testators
Baker	44
Baxster	2
Baxter	605

Again, the surname Baxter is by far the more common of the two.

For the nineteenth century, H B Guppy's survey has been mentioned above. Another important Victorian source is the *Return of Owners of Land* of 1873, sometimes known as the Modern Domesday Book. This source lists, county by county, every owner of an acre of land or more, with their residence (not necessarily the address of their property) and the acreage of their holding.

Return of Owners of Land 1873

England

Bedfordshire

Baker	7
Baxter	1

Berkshire

Bagster	1
Baker	6

Buckinghamshire

Baker	3

Cambridgeshire

Baker	12
Baxter	6

Cheshire

Baker	5
Baxter	4

Cornwall

Baker	12

Cumberland
  Baker   1
  Baxter   8
Derbyshire
  Baker   7
  Baxter   1
Devon
  Bagster   1
  Baker   42
  Baxter   2
Dorset
  Baker   12
County Durham
  Baker   2
Essex
  Baker   27
  Baster   1
  Baxter   3
Gloucestershire
  Baker   27
  Baxter   3
Hampshire
  Baker   19
Herefordshire
  Baker   15
Hertfordshire
  Baker   4
Huntingdonshire
  Baker   2
  Baxter   3
Kent
  Baker   26
  Baxter   2

Lancashire
  Baker   12
  Baxter   6
Leicestershire
  Baker   9
  Baxter   5
Lincolnshire
  Baker   28
  Baxter   14
Middlesex
  Baker   13
  Baxter   1
Monmouthshire
  Baker   24
Norfolk
  Baker   28
Northamptonshire
  Backer   1
  Baker   9
  Baxter   4
Northumberland
  Baker   1
Nottinghamshire
  Baker   10
  Baxter   1
Oxfordshire
  Baker   5
Rutlandshire
  Baker   2
Shropshire
  Baker   6
  Baxter   1
Somerset
  Baker   98

Staffordshire
  Baker   26
  Baxter   2
Suffolk
  Bacher   1
  Backer   1
  Baker   29
  Baxter   1
Surrey
  Baker   14
  Baxter   1
Sussex
  Baker   12
  Baxter   2
Warwickshire
  Baker   14
  Baxter   3
Westmorland
  Baker   1
Wiltshire
  Baker   9
Worcestershire
  Baker   19
Yorkshire East
  Baker   3
  Baxter   3
Yorkshire North
  Baker   16
  Baxter   2
Yorkshire West
  Baker   6
  Baxter   14

Wales
Denbighshire
  Baker   3
Montgomeryshire
  Baxter   3

As we can see, the Baker surname has spread to all English counties by the 1870s, as has Baxter. The three isolated appearances of the surname Baker in Wales occur in Denbighshire. Again the most common surname, of the two, is Baker.

Decennial census returns were instituted in England, Scotland and Wales in 1801. Personal returns survive from 1841 onwards, with precise ages and birthplaces given from 1851 onwards. The latest census currently available is that of 1901. The 1901, 1891, 1881, 1871, 1861 and 1851 census returns have been fully indexed. A search of all available online indexes to census returns found the following entries:

1851
Channel Islands: Baker (262); Baxter (33)
England: Backer (761); Bagster (100);
                Baiker (2); Baker (39,940); Baxster (5);
                Baxter (7243)
Isle of Man: Baker (4)
Wales: Backer (5); Bagster (2); Baker (625);
                Baxter (70)

1861
Channel Islands: Backer (4); Baker (216);
                Baxter (28)
England: Backer (712); Bagster (79);
                Baiker (4); Baker (45,155);

Baxter (8829); Baxster (5)

Isle of Man: Backer (5); Baker (3); Baxter (4)

Scotland: Backer (25); Baiker (10); Baker (258); Baxter (3323)

Wales: Backer (9); Bagster (5); Baker (802); Baxter (74)

1871

Channel Islands: Baiker (1); Baker (287); Baxter (18)

England: Backer (782); Bagster (72); Baiker (2); Baker (51,481); Baxter (9876)

Isle of Man: Baker (6); Baxter (6)

Scotland: Backer (4); Bagster (1); Baker (337); Baxter (3633)

Wales: Backer (11); Baker (1212); Baxter (88)

1881

Channel Islands: Baker (218); Baxter (21)

England: Backer (172); Bagster (79); Baiker (7); Baker (63,260); Baxter (13,384); Baxster (4)

Isle of Man: Baker (6); Baxter (2)

Scotland: Backer (9); Baiker (1); Baker (450); Baxter (4276)

Wales: Backer (2); Bagster (5); Baker (1676); Baxter (140)

1891

Channel Islands: Baker (247); Baxter (19)

England: Backer (802); Bagster (55); Baiker (6); Baker (65,169); Baxter (13,002); Baxster (1)

Isle of Man: Baker (12)

Scotland:	Backer (7); Bagster (1); Baiker (2);
	Baker (575); Baxter (4782)
Wales:	Backer (10); Bagster (4); Baker (2194);
	Baxter (97)

1901

Channel Islands:	Baker (247); Baxter (21)
England:	Backer (752); Bagster (37);
	Baiker (5); Baker (75,413);
	Baxter (15,268); Baxster (3)
Isle of Man:	Baker (4); Baxter (3)
Scotland:	Backer (7); Bagster (1);
	Baker (639); Baxter (5005)
Wales:	Backer (18); Bagster (3); Baker (2655);
	Baxter (181)

Again Baker is the most common of the two surnames (and their variants) except in Scotland where Baxter is found in greater numbers in all available census indexes.

Printed Genealogies

We found no references to printed genealogies, in the indexes we consulted, for families named Bagster, Baiker or Backer, but the following references were noted for Baker and Bax(s)ter:

Baker
Burke's *Peerage and Baronetage* 1956
Burke's *Extinct and Dormant Baronetage*
Burke's *Landed Gentry* 1863, 1894, 1921, 1937, 1952, 1965, 1969
Burke's *Irish Family Records* 1976
Burke's *Distinguished Families of the USA*
Burke's *Colonial Gentry*
Burke's *Authorised Arms*
Burke's *Visitation of Seat and Arms*, i 18
Burke's *Royal Families* (London 1851) i 78
Betham, *Baronetage*, iv 14, 363
Edward Hasted, *Kent*, ii 281; iii 49
Morant, *Essex*, i 231, 258,301,303
Berry, *Hertfordshire Genealogies*, 83, 87
Berry, *Kent Genealogies*, 216, 353
Berry, Sussex Genealogies, 225
Lewys Dwnn, *Heraldic Visitations of Wales and part of the Marches, between the years 1586 and 1613*, i 284
Sir T Phillipps, *Visitations of Berkshire*, 4
Hutchins, *Dorset*, iv 93
Surtees Society Publications: *Durham*, i 121; ii 358
The Transactions of the Thoroton Society: *Nottinghamshire*, ii 251
Metcalfe, *Visitation of Worcester*, 1683, 5

Norfolk Archaeological Society, *Visitations of Norfolk*, i 45

Howard, *Visitation of England and Wales*, vii 156; xx 53

J L Vivian, *The Visitations of Devon*, 61

Harleian Society iv 36; xiii 145; xiv 544; xv 39, 42; xxviii 21; xxxii 11; xlii 63, 178; liii 101; liv 6, 7; lvi 161, 163; lxv 6; lxxxix 5, 6; xci 8; xcii 13

George Lipscombe, *History & Antiquities of the County of Buckingham*, iv 530

Sir C Sharp, *History of Hartlepool* (1816) 83

J E Cussans, *History of Hertfordshire* (1870-1881) pts ix, x. 144

Sir J A Bradney, *The History of Monmouthshire* ...(1907-1932) i 177

Collections Historical and Archaeological relating to Montgomeryshire and its Borders (Powys Land Club) xxv 40

Transactions of the East Hertfordshire Archaeological Society vi 184

J R Scott, *Scott of Scot's Hall*, 207

G T Clark, *Genealogies of Morgan and Glamorgan*, 475

T Y Baker, *A Memoir of the Family of Baker* (Westminster, 1878)

F A Baker, *The Baker and Smart Pedigrees* (1902)

R Baker-Gabb *The Families of Baker, of Bailey-Baker and Baker-Gabb* (1903)

The Sewells of the Isle of Wight 129

Thistlethwaite Family i 200

P C Yorke ,*The Diary of John Baker* (1931) vii

F H Suckling, *A Forgotten Past* (1898) 83, 86

G C Williamson, *Family Pedigrees* (1914) – pedigree of Trehearne

H Robertson, *Stemmata Robertson et Durdin* (1895) 223

41

J Leete & J C Anderson, *The Family of Leete* (1906) 98

The Genealogist, v 230

The Genealogist, New Series, xiii 252; xxxiv 207

The Genealogical Quarterly volume 23-32

Genealogists' Magazine ix 304; xii 71

C C Brookes *A History of Steeple Aston and Middle Aston, Oxfordshire* (1929) 191

W Rye, *Norfolk Families* (1915) 455

B Buckler, *Stemmata Chicheleana: Supplement* (1775) 16, 76

Notes and Queries, 1st series, ii 67, 244; 6th series, xii 89; 12th series, vi 75, 139; cxlviii 402

Foster, *Collectanea Genealogica* (Funeral Certificates of Ireland) 10

New England Register, xliii 279

Botfield, *Stemmata Botevillian* 147

Miscelleanea Genealogica et Heraldica 5th series ix 269

Ruvigny, *Clarence Volume,* 360, 581

Ruvigny, *Exeter Volume,* 161, 470

Ruvigny, *Essex Volume,* 551, 644

Ruvigny, *Mortimer Percy Volume,* 102, 444

The Victoria County History of Hertfordshire

J B Braithwaite, *Who Are We? Notes on the Ancestry of Joseph Bevan and Martha Braithwaite* (1927)

A C Benson, *Genealogy of the Family of Benson of Banger House and Northwoods in the Parish of Ripon, County Yorkshire* (1895)

E A Loftus, *A History of the Descendants of Maximilian Cole of Oxford* (1938) 8

W A Copinger, *The Manors of Suffolk: Notes on Their History and Devolution* (1905-1911) i 391; iv 36

G C B Poulter, *The Corbould Genealogy* (1935) 71

Sir E R Pearce-Edgcumbe, *Family Records relating to the Families of Peace of Holsworthy, Edgcumbe of Laneast, Eliot of Lostwithiel, Livingstone of Calendar, Reynolds of Exeter, Gayer of Liskeard, and others* (1895) 97

Robert Thoroton, *The Antiquities of Nottinghamshire* (London, 1677) 244; (London, 1790) ii 251

Baxter

Burke's *Peerage & Baronetage* 1872, 1926

Burke's *Landed Gentry* 1921, 1965

Norfolk Archaeological Society *Visitations of Norfolk* i, 397

Foster's *Visitations of Yorkshire,* 316

Foster's *Visitations of Northumberland,* 11

Burke's *Visitations of Seats & Arms,* i 31

Rev Joseph Hunter *The History and Topography of the Deanery of Doncaster* (London 1828-1831,) i 384

Surtees Society iii 292; cxxii 59; cxxxiii 67; cxlvi 98

Harleian Society xvi 15; xxxii 23, 24

Harleian Society *Visitations of Suffolk* 1664, lxi 49

Harleian Society *Visitations of Norfolk* 1664, lxxxv 17

Notes & Queries 1st series ii 89, 206

Metcalfe *Visitations of Northamptonshire* 165

A History of Northumberland issued under the Direction of the Northumberland County History Committee (1893-1940), x 154; xi 139

Transactions of the Shropshire Archaeological Society 4th series ix 127, 141; x 119 et seq

Baxster

Miscelleanea Genealogica et Heraldica 5th series, ix 188

Heraldry

As expected, we found a great many entries for coats of arms granted to men of the name Baker, some of which we list here.

Baker of Loventor, Devon – baronet
Baker of Claives and Hilll Court, Worcester
Baker of Upper Dunstable House, Surrey – baronet
Baker of Modbury, Devon
Baker late Littlehale of Ranston, Dorset, and
    Ashcombe, Sussex – baronet
Baker of Wattisfield and Wrentham, Suffolk
Baker of Kent
Baker of Chester
Baker of Whitburn, County Durham
Baker of Elemore Hall and Crook Hall, County
    Durham
Baker of Monckwith, Essex
Baker of Exeter
Baker of Sissinghurst, Kent
Baker of Thorngrove, Worcester, and Lypeat Park,
    Gloucestershire
Baker of Waresley, Worcestershire
Baker of Worcestershire and Gloucestershire
Baker of Kent
Baker of Kent and Sussex
Baker of Lincolnshire and Smallborough, Norfolk
Baker of London, granted 1702
Baker of Derby
Baker of Northfield, Worcestershire and London
Baker of Somerset
Baker of West Hay, Somerset

Baker quartered by Addison John Baker Cresswell of
  Cresswell, Northumberland
Baker of Elemore, County Durham
Baker (Wingfield-Baker of Orset Hall, Essex)
Baker (Benjamin Baker of Miltown, Queen's County,
  Ireland)
Baker of Awsworth, Nottinghamshire
Baker of London and Worcestershire
Baker of Walton, Norfolk
Baker alias Lloyd of Terington, Norfolk
Baker of Northumberland
Baker of Radnorshire
Baker of Salisbury, Wiltshire
Baker of Shrewsbury
Baker of Well, Somerset
Baker originally of Battle, Sussex
Baker of Lismacue, County Tipperary
Baker of Fort William, County Cork
Baker of London
Baker of Feckenham, Worcestershire
Baker of Bayfordbury, Hertfordshire
Baker of Elemore, County Durham, Stanton,
  Northumberland and Boulley, Yorkshire
Baker of Aldesworth, Nottinghamshire
Baker of Bowden, Cheshire, London and Windsor
Baker of New Windsor, Berkshire
Baker of Loventor, Devon
Baker of Caldham, Kent and Calais, #France
Baker of Skerton House, Lancaster
Baker of Upper Dunstable House, Surrey

Summary

To conclude, the name Baker is of Old English origin stemming from an occupational name which has developed into one of the most common English surnames. Although Baxter is the form which grew, from the same root, in the more northern counties and in Scotland, Baker has been more successful in spreading to all areas of the British Isles, including the Isle of Man, Ireland and the Channel Islands, and Wales where occupational surnames are not common.

Sources Consulted

P H Reaney, *The Origins of English Surnames* (London: Routledge & Kegan Paul 1967)

P H Reaney & R M Wilson, *Dictionary of British Surnames* (London: Oxford, 3rd edition, 1995)

P H Reaney, *Dictionary of British Surnames* (London: Routledge & Kegan Paul, 2nd edition, 1976)

P Hanks & F Hodges, *A Dictionary of Surnames* (Oxford University Press, 1988)

M A Lower, *Patronymica Brittanica* (London, 1860)

C W Bardsley, *Dictionary of English and Welsh Surnames* (1901: reprinted, Baltimore: Genealogical Publishing Co, 1967)

C L'Estrange Ewen, *Guide to the Origin of British Surnames* (London: John Gifford, 1938)

H B Guppy, *Homes of Family Names in Great Britain* (London, 1890)

Ernest Weekley, *The Romance of Names* (London: John Murray, 2nd edition, 1917)

Ernest Weekley, *Surnames* (London: John Murray, 1917)

George F Black, *The Surnames of Scotland* (New York Public Library, 1946)

Edward MacLysaght, *The Surnames of Ireland* (Dublin: Irish University Press, 1977)

Edward MacLysaght, *Guide to Irish Surnames* (Dublin: Helicon, 1965)

Sir Robert Matheson, *Special Report on Surnames in Ireland* (1909)

T J & Prys Morgan, *Welsh Surnames* (Cardiff: University of Wales Press, 1985)

J J Kneen, *The Personal Names of the Isle of Man* (Oxford, 1937)

F K & S Hitching, *References to English Surnames in 1601* (Walton on Thames: Bernau, 1910)

F K & S Hitching, *References to English Surnames in 1602* (Walton on Thames: Bernau, 1911)

Colin D Rogers, *The Surname Detective* (Manchester, 1995)

The Concise Dictionary of National Biography, Part II, 1901-1950,
(Oxford, 1961)

Burke's Family Index (London: Burke's Peerage Limited, 1976)

H R Moulton, *Palaeography, Genealogy & Topography* (1930)

Index to Prerogative Court of Canterbury Wills (online)

G W Marshall, *The Genealogist's Guide* (1903; reprinted,
Baltimore: GPC, 1973)

J B Whitmore, *A Genealogical Guide* (London, 1953)

Charles Bridge, *An Index to Pedigrees* (London, 1867)

Geoffrey B Barrow, *The Genealogist's Guide* (London: Research
Publishing Co, 1977)

Sir Bernard Burke, *The General Armory* (London, 1884)

C R Humphrey-Smith ed, *Burke's General Armory Volume II,*
(Tabard Press, 1973)

The Return of Owners of Land (1873)

W J Hardy & W Page, *A Calendar to the Feet of Fines for London
and Middlesex: Vol 1 Richard I- Richard III (1189-1485)*
(London, 1892)

Richard McKinley, *The Surnames of Oxford,* (Leopards Head
Press, 1977)

Richard McKinley, *The Surnames of Sussex,* (Leopards Head
Press, 1988)

Richard McKinley, *The Surnames of Lancashire,* (Leopards Head
Press, 1981)

Richard McKinley, *The Surnames of Norfolk and Suffolk,*
(Phillimore, 1975)

David Postles, *The Surnames of Devon* (Leopards Head Press,
1995)

George Redmonds, *The Surnames of Yorkshire West Riding,*
(Phillimore, 1973)

R A McKinley, *A History of British Surnames* (Longman, 1990)

Mr Avenell, *The Norman People,* (London, 1874)

L G Pine, *They Came With the Conqueror* (Evans, 1954)

Elsdon C Smith, *American Surnames* (GPC, 1969)

Indexes to Census Returns for England and Wales, 1841 to 1901 (*Ancestry.com*)

Online index to Scottish Baptisms, Births, Banns, Marriages and Deaths (ScotlandsPeople)

Online index to 1861, 1871, 1881, 1891 and 1901 census for Scotland (ScotlandsPeople)

Indexes to Scottish Wills and Testaments (*ScotlandsPeople*) 1513-1901